Live Better

crystal therapy

Live Better

crystal therapy

exercises and inspirations
for well-being

SHIRLEY O'DONOGHUE

DUNCAN BAIRD PUBLISHERS
LONDON

Live Better: Crystal Therapy
Shirley O'Donoghue

First published in the United Kingdom
and Ireland in 2007 by
Duncan Baird Publishers Ltd
Sixth Floor, Castle House
75–76 Wells Street
London W1T 3QH

Conceived, created and designed by
Duncan Baird Publishers

Managing Editor: Kelly Thompson
Editor: Ingrid Court-Jones
Editorial Assistant: Kirty Topiwala
Managing Designer: Daniel Sturges
Picture Researcher: Louise Glasson
Commissioned photography: Matthew Ward

British Library Cataloguing-in-Publication Data:
A CIP record for this book is available from the
British Library.

10 9 8 7 6 5 4 3 2 1

ISBN: 978-1-84483-390-0

Typeset in Filosofia and Son Kern
Colour reproduction by Scanhouse, Malaysia
Printed and bound in Malaysia by Imago

Publisher's notes

Before following any advice or practice suggested
in this book, it is recommended that you consult
your doctor as to its suitability, especially if
you suffer from any health problems or special
conditions. The publishers and the author
cannot accept any responsibility for any injuries
or damage incurred as a result of following
the exercises in this book, or of using any
of the therapeutic methods described or
mentioned here.

The abbreviations BCE and CE are used throughout
this book. BCE means Before the Common Era
(equivalent to BC); CE means of the Common Era
(equivalent to AD).

contents

Introduction 6

Chapter One

Origins and basics 8
• What is crystal therapy? 10 • How crystals form 12 • Crystals through the ages 14
• Common crystal forms 16 • Core crystal directory 18 • Red jasper/Carnelian 20
• Golden tiger's eye/Rose quartz 22 • Blue lace agate/Sodalite 24 • Amethyst/Clear
quartz 26 • How to choose crystals 28 • Looking after your crystals 30 • Therapist
or self-treatment? 32 • Inspirations 34

Chapter Two

How crystals work 36
• The power of chi 38 • Discover your chi 40 • The chakras 42 • Chakras at a glance 44
• The power of colour 46 • Colour associations 48 • How to enhance crystal energy 50
• Experiencing crystal energy 52 • Crystal placements 54 • Making gem essences 56
• Inspirations 58

Chapter Three

Balancing the chakras 60
• Stress and imbalance in the body 62 • The importance of being grounded 64
• Realizing your goals 66 • Finding contentment 68 • Harnessing your strength 70
• Giving unconditional love 72 • Finding your own voice 74 • Getting in touch with
your intuition 76 • Becoming spiritually aware 78 • Harmonizing your chakras 80
• Overcoming "dis-ease" 82 • Inspirations 84

Chapter Four

Directing crystal energy 86
• Protecting your energy 88 • Increasing your energy 90 • Receiving love and
nurturing 92 • Setting positive aims 94 • Boosting self-confidence 96 • Resolving
problems 98 • Finding clarity 100 • Tapping in to calm 102 • Aiding effective
communication 104 • Enhancing creativity 106 • Inspirations 108

Chapter Five

Expanding your work with crystals 110
• Crystals in the home 112 • Children and crystals 114 • Pets and crystals 116
• Crystals in the workplace 118 • Crystals as gifts: birthstones 120 • Crystals and other
therapies 122 • Inspirations 124

Index 126
Credits and acknowledgments 128

INTRODUCTION

Crystals quite simply changed my life. When I began using crystals over 12 years ago, I was intrigued by the energy that I could feel from them. I started a crystal healing course as a hobby, but by the end of the first year I was teaching crystal healing at a college, despite having no teaching experience and a deep-rooted fear of public speaking! Since then, crystals have opened up all sorts of doors for me to step through, both on a personal and professional level.

Although I now practise a wide range of complementary therapies, I still find crystal therapy the most effective treatment in terms of the mind, body and spirit as a whole. I've introduced many people to crystal therapy and I'm always amazed at the beneficial effects that crystals have on their lives – from improving relationships and boosting self-esteem to easing pain and illness. Crystals have an uncanny ability to open us up to all sorts of possibilities.

In recent years, crystals have become increasingly easier to obtain, and public awareness of crystal therapy has grown enormously. This developing interest is very encouraging, because it means that the power of crystals is reaching an ever-growing audience.

However, in my experience, many people still purchase crystals solely on the basis of their decorative qualities without realizing how the stones could enhance their lives. Others are overwhelmed by the sheer choice of crystals available and are therefore unable to select them according to their own needs. This is why *Live Better Crystal Therapy* is so useful – it's the perfect introduction to a range of key crystals, and the techniques that will help you to use them.

I hope that this book will encourage you to tap into the infinite possibilities offered by crystals for your own personal and spiritual development. All that is required is an open mind. The crystals will do the rest!

origins and basics

Created by chemical processes during movements of the Earth's crust over millions of years, crystals have always fascinated humankind. With their captivating colours and extraordinary forms, they have been coveted as beautiful ornaments and adornments throughout history. But our early ancestors also sensed that the stones had "magical" powers, and regarded them as gifts from the spirits in the heavens. Research in recent times has enabled us to better understand these "magical" powers as energetic qualities, which vary from stone to stone.

Crystal therapy is a way of harnessing this crystal energy to enhance our lives – not only our physical health and well-being, but also our emotional and spiritual welfare. And this book is the perfect introduction to bringing crystal therapy into your life.

In this chapter, we begin by exploring the unique natural process by which crystals are created, before going on to discuss their different forms and how they have been used and revered over the ages. We then go on to introduce you to eight key crystals (and their main qualities). This will help you to choose from the dazzling array of stones available these days, as well as to obtain the full benefit from this book. And finally, there is advice on how to cleanse, store and look after your crystals.

WHAT IS CRYSTAL THERAPY?

Crystal therapy is a holistic treatment that works by activating the body's own healing mechanisms to bring us physically, mentally, emotionally and spiritually back into balance. But how can crystals do this?

Scientists discovered long ago that crystals have a stable internal structure of perfectly repeating patterns. Many crystals also emit a piezoelectrical charge – this means that they vibrate and generate energy. One theory as to how crystal therapy works is that, because of the perfect structure of crystals, their vibrations increase harmony in their immediate environment by restoring the energy fields of any people present to their optimal states. Crystal therapists harness these vibrations and the therapeutic properties of the stones' colours (see pp.46–7) to re-tune and rebalance the body's energy systems to their individual blueprint for perfect health.

A crystal therapy treatment normally starts with a conversation between the therapist and the client, during which they discuss the latter's medical history and why the person has come for therapy. All information about the client is kept completely confidential. Then, the client lies on a couch or sits in a chair fully clothed, and the therapist reads their subtle energy system by holding a crystal pendulum or his or her hands about two inches (5cm) above the client's body.

Our subtle energy system (see pp.40–43) is made up of the aura (a sheath of energy surrounding the body), the meridians (channels that distribute subtle energy around the body) and the chakras (spinning vortices of energy located at seven points between the base of the spine and the crown of the head). Other common terms for subtle energy are *chi*, *prana* and life force.

During the treatment, the therapist chooses and places crystals around, and occasionally on, the client's body to correct the energy imbalances they perceive, keeping the stones in place for 10 to 30 minutes.

After the treatment, the therapist makes sure that the client feels grounded (firmly anchored in the physical world) again. Most recipients report a deep sense of peace and relaxation during and after crystal therapy.

HOW CRYSTALS FORM

Most of the crystals used in crystal therapy have taken millions of years to form. But how? Movement in the Earth's crust forces molten rock, hot liquids and gases from the mantle below to rise closer to the surface, where they cool and harden to make "igneous" rock.

Crystals form in this rock when the pressure, temperature and minerals provide ideal conditions for the rock to crystallize. The type and colour of the crystals are determined largely by the chemical composition of the minerals present in the rock and the amount of space they have available in which to grow.

When igneous rock and crystals are exposed at the Earth's surface, they are eroded to dust by the elements. This dust is washed down rivers to the sea and deposited as silt. Over millions of years the silt compresses to reform as "sedimentary" rock and crystals. If igneous or sedimentary rocks and crystals undergo further changes from pressure and heat, their particles may re-combine into "metamorphic" rock and new crystals.

CRYSTALS THROUGH THE AGES

Throughout history, many civilizations have used crystals, whether as symbols of power, evidence of status and wealth, symbols of love and affection, amulets for protection, or as tools for initiation and healing. For example, crystals have historical associations with many religions. In the Bible, Aaron, the first priest of the Israelites, is described as having carnelians in his breastplate, and angels gave King Solomon a ring of crystals representing the four elements: earth, air, fire and water. Islam has the Black Stone of Mecca, which is touched by all pilgrims and which Muslims consider to be the right hand of God on Earth.

The first recorded evidence of "healing" crystals is in an Egyptian papyrus dating from around 1600BCE, which gives instructions for using crystals therapeutically. The Egyptians made necklaces of lapis lazuli, malachite and red jasper for sick people to wear, believing that the stones would help to banish their illnesses. They also ground down lapis lazuli, and even used it in a surgical procedure known as "trepanning" — implanting the crystal in the forehead at the brow chakra (see p.45), to encourage the person to develop psychic skills.

The ancient Greeks, too, recognized the holistic healing properties of crystals, as did many other civilizations over the centuries, including the Mayans, the Celts, the Native North Americans and the Aborigines. During the 16th century, wealthy Europeans even took ground crystal powders as curative medicines.

When in 1746 the English apothecary and author Sir John Hill wrote that it was the minerals in crystals that accounted for their healing properties, he was echoing the more scientific approach that was becoming more prevalent in medicine at that time. Soon, doctors just treated the symptoms of illness rather than treating the person as a whole, as they had done previously.

It was not until the 1980s that Marcel Vogel, an American research scientist, carried out pioneering work that suggested it was the perfect structure of the crystals that could heal through their ability to store, amplify, convert and repair subtle energy.

COMMON CRYSTAL FORMS

While the basic atomical structure of crystals is always the same, the stones come in many different shapes and forms – some natural and some man-made. The most useful forms for crystal therapy are listed below.

Chunks

This form looks just like a lump of rock. Exuding a soft, diffuse energy, it is good for absorbing electromagnetic stress from computers and other office equipment. Chunks are relatively inexpensive to buy from crystal retailers. Rose quartz is particularly common in this form.

Clusters

Clusters are formed by groups of small crystals that join together. They are particularly good at radiating energizing, calming or cleansing energy into any room or environment, depending on the type of crystal you use. Crystals that commonly grow as clusters are amethyst and clear quartz.

Tumblestones

Tumblestones are created by tumbling small crystals in a special machine with an abrasive until they become smooth and shiny. Most crystals are available in this form, which makes them both inexpensive and convenient to carry around. You can place a stone in your pocket to keep its energy with you wherever you go, or to act as a useful reminder of something important every time you touch it.

Shaped and faceted crystals

Crystals are sometimes cut and polished into shapes, such as spheres, pyramids, obelisks and hearts, which makes them very attractive as orna-ments. If stones are cut well, their energy is amplified by their shape. For example, a sphere has a protective quality, while a heart shape projects love.

CORE CRYSTAL DIRECTORY

To encourage you to experience the way that crystals work, we present in the following pages eight core crystals: red jasper, carnelian, golden tiger's eye, rose quartz, blue lace agate, sodalite, amethyst and clear quartz. They are all easy to obtain, offer a range of healing energies and form a good basis from which to build up your crystal collection. They are all also members of the quartz family, so they have a rating of seven on the Mohs Scale — a comparative scale of the hardness of stones. This means that they are robust enough to be carried around in your pocket. You can also cleanse them all safely by washing them in water (see pp.30–31).

Each core crystal entry lists the crystal's main qualities and associations, including its related chakra. And we also suggest one or more alternative stones in each case, which can be used to treat the same chakra's energy. This provides you with an added element of choice, as it is important to work with the crystals to which you are most drawn (see pp.28–9).

RED JASPER

Chakra: base

Key qualities: protective, grounding, focusing

Red jasper prevents the absorption of negative and distracting energies, supporting our ability to focus, and encouraging us to complete projects. A very common crystal, it also stimulates our enthusiasm and enhances our drive to achieve our desired goals in life.

The Native North Americans considered red jasper to be a sacred stone and their shamans often used it to provide protection against negativity.

Alternatives

- *Smoky quartz*: absorbs negative energy
- *Hematite*: offers emotional protection; empowers

CARNELIAN

Chakra: sacral

Key qualities: warming, harmonizing, stabilizing

Carnelian is a strong orange colour and has a vibrant, warming energy that helps us to feel secure and level-headed. It also has a protective quality, which helps to promote courage and a sense of being on solid ground.

The ancient Egyptians placed carnelian amulets on the dead, so that the goddess Isis would grant them a safe passage on their journey to the afterlife.

Alternatives

- *Orange calcite*: energizes and cleanses
- *Moonstone*: supports women's health, particularly during menstruation and pregnancy

GOLDEN TIGER'S EYE

Chakra: solar plexus

Key qualities: practical, soothing, empowering

Tiger's eye has a masculine energy, which is particularly good for helping to increase and support personal power, and to aid clear thinking. It is available in red, brown, black and blue, as well as in gold.

When polished, the stone reflects a narrow band of light that seems to change position as you move it – an effect called chatoyancy, after the French for "cat's eye".

Alternatives

- *Yellow jasper*: a steadying influence, which helps to foster positive thinking
- *Citrine*: uplifts and helps to manifest abundance

ROSE QUARTZ

Chakra: heart

Key qualities: loving, calming, releasing

Beautiful rose quartz ranges in colour from soft, milky pink to lavender pink. This crystal fosters a sense of self-worth and a sincere appreciation of others, as well as generating a feeling of relaxation.

You will usually find it as chunks, tumblestones, or fashioned into shapes such as wands, hearts and obelisks. Clusters are rare and therefore expensive.

Alternatives

- *Green aventurine*: good for balancing emotions related to relationships
- *Green calcite*: helps to release old, limiting beliefs

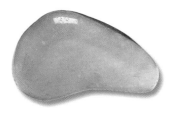

BLUE LACE AGATE

Chakra: throat

Key qualities: opening, cooling, nurturing

With its delicate, blue-and-white lacy patterning, this crystal promotes calm self-expression, so it aids public speaking and also helps to make discussions run more smoothly by encouraging kindness and understanding.

In ancient times, agate was credited with many healing powers, including the ability to improve eyesight, lessen thirst and bring faithfulness to relationships.

Alternatives

- *Aquamarine*: brings tranquillity and creative inspiration
- *Blue calcite*: aids communication in resolving differences of opinion

SODALITE

Chakra: brow

Key qualities: creative, instinctive, cleansing

Sodalite is good for balancing logical and intuitive thought processes, which can help to solve all sorts of problems. It also encourages inventive thinking, as it promotes fresh ideas and innovations.

This stone is often confused with lapis lazuli, which looks similar. However, you can tell them apart because lapis lazuli contains golden threads of pyrite.

Alternatives

- *Lapis lazuli*: encourages insight into the subconscious realm, such as dreams and intuition
- *Apophyllite*: connects the physical and spiritual planes

AMETHYST

Chakra: crown

Key qualities: healing, integrating, spiritual

With its particularly powerful and protective qualities, amethyst can quickly rebalance energy. It is an effective stone to encourage greater spiritual awareness when meditating, and it can also be used to aid restful sleep.

Often worn by royalty, amethyst also has religious associations. In the West it is worn by Christian bishops, while in Tibet it is considered sacred to the Buddha.

Alternatives

- *Celestite*: stimulates a connection to divine realms
- *Selenite*: encourages deep meditation and peace

CLEAR QUARTZ

Chakras: all, particularly crown
Key qualities: absorbing, purifying, balancing

Although therapists use clear quartz with all the chakras, they most often work with it on the crown chakra. Clear quartz can intensify and amplify intentions on all levels, but it also has a strong clarifying, purifying quality.

Quartz has been used for thousands of years by many civilizations for religious and medicinal purposes. Today, we often harness its piezoelectrical energy to stabilize frequencies in computers, clocks, security cameras, radio transmitters and so on.

Alternative

· *Herkimer diamond*: aids focus and detoxification

HOW TO CHOOSE CRYSTALS

Choosing crystals is an intuitive process and the best way to do it is simply to allow your eye to be drawn to a particular stone. Some people use a pendulum to dowse crystals, some "scan" with their hands to feel the crystals' energies, and others like to handle them. Whatever method you employ, it's best not to spend too much time on the process. Making a quick choice allows you to listen to the right, intuitive side of your brain before the left, logical side of your brain starts to interfere with rational thoughts, such as "But I don't like blue!" or "Why do I want that one?".

Colour plays an important part in choosing crystals, not only because it can cause you to be visually attracted to a particular stone, but also because colour conveys vital information about the crystal's energetic qualities to you on a subconscious level (see pp.46–9)

When choosing crystals it is also a good idea to focus on your intended purpose for them – for example, whether you want to use them to attract love or to release stress. The core crystal directory (see pp.18–27) will help you with this. If you are choosing crystals for someone else, try visualizing the person during the selection process. Always trust your instincts and choose the crystal(s) to which you are first drawn.

However, if you discover that you really dislike a certain crystal, it is worth finding out more about its qualities and potentially working with it. This is because an aversion to a certain colour or crystal can be an indication that your energy flow in the areas related to that colour or crystal is impaired and needs rebalancing.

LOOKING AFTER YOUR CRYSTALS

Crystals absorb (and store) both positive and negative energy from their surroundings, as well as from anyone who picks them up or even walks past them. For this reason you should "cleanse" your crystals regularly.

Many stones, such as members of the quartz family, to which all the core crystals in this book belong (see pp.18–27), can be cleansed by washing them in ordinary or salt water. However, water can damage some stones, so unless you know for certain that your crystals are impervious to it, it is best to use the gentler method of burning incense near them. Alternatively, you can use the ancient Native North American technique of "smudging" by burning sage leaves so that the smoke from the leaves purifies the crystals. Another good method for cleansing them is to close your eyes and simply imagine breathing white light onto them. You can even use sound to purify crystals by sounding a bell close to them.

Knowing the hardness ratings of your crystals according to the Mohs Scale (see p.18) will enable you to keep hard and soft stones apart, thus avoiding damaging them. In 1812, the German mineralogist Friedrich Mohs devised this scale, which we still use today. Its principle is simple: the lower the rating, the softer the crystal. For example, talc, the softest substance, is rated at 1 on the Mohs Scale, while diamond, the hardest, is rated at 10.

If you only have a few crystals, wrap them individually in tissue paper or pieces of soft fabric to protect them, and then keep them in a small bag or box. Then, if you go on to expand your collection, you might wish to invest in a large box with separate compartments for the crystals, to ensure that the harder ones don't scratch the softer ones. DIY stores sell inexpensive containers for different sizes of nails, screws and so on, which are ideal for storing a crystal collection. They usually have a transparent lid, which makes it easy to find a particular crystal quickly, while at the same time protecting the stones from dust. However, take care not to expose your crystals to direct sunlight for long periods of time – many stones, including amethyst and rose quartz, fade when left in sunlight.

THERAPIST OR SELF-TREATMENT?

When you first work with crystals, it is a good idea to visit a professional therapist who can explain every step of the treatment, as well as support your responses to it, and provide insight and encouragement.

In fact, even experienced crystal therapists often prefer to be treated by another therapist rather than treat themselves. When a practitioner is giving a treatment, you can relax fully in the knowledge that they are monitoring your energy field and moving or changing crystals as necessary. The treatment is also more powerful because the therapist's energy boosts the energy of the crystals.

Always make sure that your crystal therapist has been properly trained and is fully insured. In the UK, the Affiliation of Crystal Healing Organizations (ACHO) have a list of all crystal therapists who have been trained in accordance with the ACHO curriculum and who are appropriately insured. Similar lists are available in the USA from the Association of Melody Crystal Healing

Instructors and the Crystal Academy of Advanced Healing Arts, which train and accredit therapists.

Of course, self-treatment has its own benefits, too. These include being able to enjoy crystal therapy on an *ad hoc* basis – whenever you feel you need it most, in the comfort of your own home and at a time of day that is convenient. You also don't need to pay yourself!

When opting for self-treatment, it is best to wear loose, comfortable clothes. Keep the room warm and the lighting subdued – candlelight is a good choice. You could also burn incense to keep the energy in the room pure or burn calming essential oils, such as frankincense or jasmine. Soothing background music can help you to relax, but make sure that it lasts as long as the treatment – if the music stops suddenly, it is likely to disturb you.

To give yourself a treatment, sit fully clothed on a chair or lie on the floor with your crystals around you or in your hand (see pp.88–105). You could keep a blanket to hand as body temperature usually drops during therapy. A blanket also provides a feeling of protection, which aids the effectiveness of the treatment.

Everything in nature contains all the powers of nature.
Everything is made of one hidden stuff.

RALPH WALDO EMERSON

(1803–82)

I believe that there is a subtle magnetism in Nature,
which, if we unconsciously yield to it,
will direct us aright.

HENRY DAVID THOREAU

(1817–62)

Chapter Two

how crystals work

By now, we know that crystals transmit and are able to absorb and transmute electromagnetic energy. Their colour and vibrations affect us physically, emotionally, mentally and spiritually by rebalancing our body's vital energy flow or *chi*, thus restoring us to our natural state of well-being.

In this chapter, we look more closely at *how* this comes about. We start by learning how to recognize our own *chi*, and go on to explore the subtle energy system in greater depth, discovering more about the chakras — the spinning wheels of energy that connect the physical body to the subtle body. Next, we learn how to assess which chakras we need to focus on, and which crystals and chakras work best together. Building on the information given in Chapter 1 (see pp.18–29), this chapter offers further help in choosing the right crystals to work with – for example, by gauging whether our chakras have deficient, excess or balanced energy, or by picking crystals of a certain colour.

We then go on to consider how to make crystals work more effectively, such as through approaching them with a positive intent, harnessing deep breathing and employing visualizations. And finally, we look at some of the more advanced techniques of working with crystals, such as using placements and making gem essences.

THE POWER OF CHI

Many Eastern disciplines, such as yoga, tai chi and chi gung, are based on the premise that we all have an invisible or subtle energy, which permeates our physical body. Known as *chi*, *qi*, *prana* or the universal life force, this energy is transported around the body in channels called meridians, akin to a river and its tributaries. This same subtle energy also surrounds our physical bodies, forming what is called the aura or bio-magnetic sheath.

To maintain our health and well-being, *chi* needs to be able to flow smoothly around our bodies, but many different aspects of our lives can affect it adversely. For example, an overly sedentary lifestyle, negative thought patterns and constant stress can all cause blockages and imbalances in the flow of *chi*. This often manifests itself as a feeling of being "out of sorts" or even as an illness.

Crystal therapy has the capacity to unblock and rebalance the flow of *chi* in the body by readjusting it and returning it to its natural, optimal level. This, in turn, restores us to vibrant health and well-being.

DISCOVER YOUR CHI

Before you can use crystals to rebalance your *chi*, you first need to learn to tune in to your own subtle energy. The following exercise, which is used by many martial arts teachers, will enable you to start doing this.

Gently rub your hands together and then draw them apart to about the width of a balloon. Next, close your eyes and gently "bounce" your hands against where the skin of the balloon would be. What you feel will depend on your individual energy field, but some people say that they feel resistance as they try to push their hands together, while others report a tingling sensation or draught. However you experience it, what you feel between your hands is your very own energy.

Once you have discovered your *chi*, you can experiment with how crystals are able to affect the subtle energy system. Taking one crystal at a time, rub it softly between your hands and then repeat the exercise above. The sensations you feel from each crystal will vary, as each stone will affect your energy field in a different way.

THE CHAKRAS

Your *chi* is contained within the invisible sheath of energy that surrounds your body, known as the aura. The human aura is made up of seven subtle bodies, each of which is linked to one of the seven chakras – the principal hubs of *chi*, found where meridians intersect.

We have seven main chakras, which are located on a vertical axis running from the top of the head to the base of the spine. Each of these chakras has a particular type of energy and is related to specific body parts and emotions (see pp.44–5). To visualize these chakras, imagine them as spinning wheels of energy.

In a healthy person, these energy centres are reasonably well balanced and aligned. However, when the chakras become imbalanced or misaligned, we tend to feel ill and/or lose our emotional equilibrium.

For this reason, crystal therapists focus a great deal on directing energy from crystals to bring the chakras back into balance. The core crystals (see pp.18–27) have been specially chosen to work with the seven chakras.

CHAKRAS AT A GLANCE

This guide to the seven chakras will help you to decide which ones you wish to work on. For each we give its location, associated colour(s), key quality, associated crystals and the symptoms revealing its energetic state.

Base Chakra: base of spine · red · survival · red jasper, smoky quartz, hematite. *Deficient energy*: anxiety, lack of concentration. *Excess energy*: sluggishness, resistance to change. *Balanced energy*: vitality, security.

Sacral Chakra: just below navel · orange · pleasure · carnelian, orange calcite, moonstone. *Deficient energy*: fear of change, loss of libido. *Excess energy*: over-indulgence, over-sensitivity. *Balanced energy*: kindness, poise.

Solar Plexus Chakra: solar plexus · yellow · power · golden tiger's eye, citrine, yellow jasper. *Deficient energy*: low self-esteem, passivity. *Excess energy*: aggression, arrogance. *Balanced energy*: high self-esteem, sense of humour.

Heart Chakra: centre of chest · pink and green · love · rose quartz, green aventurine, green calcite. *Deficient energy*: depression, loneliness, fear of relationships. *Excess energy*: insecurity, jealousy, over-dependency. *Balanced energy*: compassion, affection, altruism.

Throat Chakra: throat · blue · communication · blue lace agate, aquamarine, blue calcite. *Deficient energy*: poor self-expression, shyness. *Excess energy*: loudness, verbosity. *Balanced energy*: good communication skills.

Brow Chakra: centre of forehead · indigo · intuition · lapis lazuli, sodalite, azurite. *Deficient energy*: poor memory and lack of imagination. *Excess energy*: lack of focus, over-active imagination. *Balanced energy*: perceptiveness, able imagination, good problem-solving skills.

Crown Chakra: brain · white, purple, gold · spirituality · amethyst, clear quartz. *Deficient energy*: apathy, greed. *Excess energy*: over-intellectualization, instability, confusion. *Balanced energy*: intelligence, thoughtfulness.

THE POWER OF COLOUR

The colour of a crystal is determined by the way in which light is absorbed by its atoms and molecules. When you pass light through a crystal, some is held within the stone and some is reflected off the surface. The colour of the crystal is determined by which light is absorbed (not seen) and which light is reflected (seen).

As crystal therapists work with a colour-based tool, they are also colour therapists. Colour can not only affect us physically, psychologically and emotionally, but also energetically, through our subtle energy system. For example, blue is cooling, while red is energizing.

By using crystals of a certain colour, therapists can address particular problems. This works especially well when rebalancing the chakras. For example, to rebalance the throat chakra, which governs communication and is linked with blue, the therapist would use a blue stone, such as blue lace agate; or to rebalance the brow chakra, the seat of intuition associated with indigo, they would use an indigo stone, such as sodalite, and so on.

COLOUR ASSOCIATIONS

Here we show the associations and qualities of various colours. These will help you to choose the crystals that represent atttributes you aspire to or wish to work on.

- **Red** (base chakra) *Associations*: fire, danger, passion. *Qualities*: hot, dynamic, intense. *Red crystals include*: red jasper, garnet, ruby and spinel.

- **Orange** (sacral chakra) *Associations*: adventure, joy. *Qualities*: warm, creative, assertive. *Orange crystals include*: carnelian, aragonite, fire opal and sunstone.

- **Yellow** (solar plexus chakra) *Associations*: health, optimism. *Qualities*: intellectual, powerful. *Yellow crystals include*: yellow jasper, tiger's eye, citrine and sulphur.

- **Green** (heart chakra) *Associations*: fertility, nature. *Qualities*: constant, passive. *Green crystals include*: aventurine, serpentine, moss agate and jade.

- **Pink** (heart chakra) *Associations*: love, femininity. *Qualities*: warm-hearted, maternal. *Pink crystals include*: rose quartz, rhodochrosite, kunzite and morganite.

- **Light Blue** (throat chakra) *Associations*: wisdom, discernment. *Qualities*: responsible, calming. *Light blue crystals include*: blue lace agate, aquamarine, turquoise and celestite.

- **Indigo** (brow chakra) *Associations*: tranquillity, confidence. *Qualities*: intuitive, creative. *Indigo crystals include*: sodalite, lapis lazuli, sapphire and azurite.

- **Purple** (crown chakra) *Associations*: dignity, luxury. *Qualities*: regal, spiritual. *Purple crystals include*: amethyst, iolite, sugilite and purple fluorite.

- **White/Clear** (all chakras) *Associations*: cleanliness, clarity. *Qualities*: honest, pure. *White/clear crystals include*: snowy quartz, selenite, howlite, clear quartz and Herkimer diamond.

HOW TO ENHANCE
CRYSTAL ENERGY

Once you have chosen your crystals, you can use a number of techniques to enjoy their full therapeutic benefits.

Positive Intent

In crystal therapy your focus or concentration is known as your "intent". It is important to start any crystal work in an upbeat frame of mind and to use your intent positively. Many people believe that our thoughts are vibrational frequencies which, when clearly directed, can make things happen on the physical plane. Thus, the clearer your intent, the more effective the process of harnessing the crystal's energy. If you feel that a crystal won't do anything, then it probably won't!

A good way to show positive intent is to use affirmations – statements that reprogramme your subconscious. Used along with crystals and creative visualization (see opposite), affirmations (see pp.94–5) can help you to create the changes you desire in your life.

Breathing

To enhance your sensitivity to crystal energy, you need to feel peaceful. A simple yet effective way to find calm is by regulating your breathing. Although we breathe automatically, we often don't take in enough oxygen because our breathing is too shallow. By breathing deeply you will not only feel calmer, but also help the body to purify the blood, benefiting both body and mind.

Visualization

This is a process in which you use your imagination to create positive mental images – a useful tool to reinforce your intent as you work with your crystals. Sit somewhere quiet and comfortable, close your eyes and empty your mind. Then, vizualize anything you wish, from being in a place where you feel relaxed and happy, such as on a beautiful beach, to enjoying the successful outcome of a situation, such as a job interview. Many sportspeople use visualizations of themselves winning events to enhance their physical performances. This technique will help you to get the most from your crystal work.

EXPERIENCING CRYSTAL ENERGY

We have looked at *how* to work with crystals so that we can reap their full benefits. Now we're going to put the techniques into practice.

Once you have selected a crystal to work with – one that you feel particularly drawn to, or which has the qualities you need (see pp.20–27) – spend a few moments using the techniques on pp.50–51 to make sure that your intent is pure and that you wish foremost to work for the highest good.

Now, holding the crystal in your right hand – the hand that traditionally gives out energy in crystal work – close your eyes and think about its positive qualities. Then, focus on how you want this crystal to help you. You could do this by creating and reciting an affirmation. For example, if you are using a rose quartz crystal with the intention of improving your relationship with your partner, you could say something such as: "This rose quartz helps me to be more loving toward myself and my partner." Then give thanks for the crystal's energies.

Keeping the crystal in your hand and your intention in mind, breathe in deeply through your nose. Feel the air descend down into your abdomen. Now feel it going out along your arms and legs to your hands and feet. Then breathe out slowly. Continue in this way for a couple of minutes or until your breathing is deeper and slower.

Still holding your crystal, repeat the breathing exercise, but this time, as you breathe in, visualize your breath as being the same colour as the crystal you are holding. As you breathe out, imagine your crystal-coloured breath flushing out any negativity from your body. Finally, imagine yourself achieving your aim. Spend time building up in your mind's eye as detailed a picture of this as you can. Use all your senses to experience your ideal outcome to the full.

Afterwards, place your crystal with items linked to your goal. For example, if you are trying to improve your relationship with your partner, put the crystal next to a photograph of him or her. This will direct the crystal's energy toward fulfilling your wish, and it will also provide inspiration and support in reaching your goal.

CRYSTAL PLACEMENTS

Crystal therapists often work with layouts of crystals, which are also known as placements, arrays, grids or nets. The therapist places the stones on or near specific parts of their clients' subtle energy system to balance or stimulate them. The client could be lying on a treatment couch or sitting on a chair with the crystals on the floor around them. During the treatment, the therapist monitors the crystals' energy by scanning the stones with their hands. Sometimes they move or replace the crystals.

Crystal therapists often use complex arrangements, but even beginners can use simple layouts. A good one to try is the rose quartz "bath" grid (see pp.92–3), which will help you to develop more love and compassion.

Another useful layout is the citrine grid (see opposite), which will both energize and empower you. Place six pieces of citrine around your body: one above your head, one by each shoulder, one by each hip and one at your feet. Then simply hold a piece of tiger's eye in your left hand. Lie in this placement for 10 to 15 minutes.

MAKING GEM ESSENCES

Experiments by the French scientist, Jacques Benveniste, in the 1990s and also, more recently, by the Japanese researcher, Dr Masaru Emoto, have confirmed that water can hold a memory or a signature of energy. Making what are called gem essences allows us to capture the vibrational signature of the crystals in liquid form.

Gem essences are available commercially, but creating your own is easy. Simply place a crystal in a bowl of sunlit spring water for a few hours so that the water absorbs the crystal's energy, and then bottle the water. Many professional producers preserve the essence by mixing the energized water with brandy.

The core crystals mentioned in this book and any members of the quartz family are ideal for making gem essences, but don't use water-soluble crystals, such as selenite and sulphur for obvious reasons, and *never* use toxic stones, such as cinnabar, which contains mercury, or orpiment, which is arsenic. If you have any doubts, always consult a mineralogical textbook or an expert.

One of the advantages of gem essences is that they allow us to receive the crystal's energy in a variety of ways. The most common way is by mouth – either as two or three drops dripped under the tongue with a small dropper, or in a glass of spring water, which you sip several times a day. Alternatively, you can add a few drops to your bathwater or add three or four drops to massage oil and rub this into your skin. Another way is to mix the gem essence with a little water, pour this into a plant sprayer and then spray it onto your aura or around the room. You can also rub a few drops on your pulse points, place a few drops on the palms of your hands and, using a sweeping motion, pass them through your aura or simply inhale the essence from your hands.

Reactions to essences vary. Some people experience an emotional response, known as a "healing reaction", as the essence releases energy. However, this usually takes place gradually and is for the ultimate good. Taking gem essences is never a substitute for medical treatment, but the essences may help to remove underlying emotional imbalances, which can help the body to heal itself.

Colour which, like music, is a matter of vibration,
reaches what is most general and therefore most
indefinable in nature: its inner power.

PAUL GAUGUIN

(1848–1903)

Chapter Three

balancing the chakras

One of the main purposes of balancing the chakras is to remove energy blockages or imbalances of a physical, emotional, mental and spiritual nature before they have a chance to manifest as illness in the physical body. Specific issues and concerns are associated with specific chakras (see pp.44–5) – for example, low self-esteem or a lack of self-confidence is linked with the solar plexus chakra. You can support or improve such problems by working with their particular chakra and their appropriate crystal(s).

In this chapter, we examine how the modern menace of stress is often a root cause of such blockages and imbalances in our bodies and we explore the importance of being grounded — that is, firmly anchored in the real world — before we attempt to rebalance ourselves.

Then, we move on to work with each chakra in turn in seven inspiring visualizations. These are an excellent way to begin to connect with and use the energy of the core crystals. Each exercise is colour-based, so it is designed to work with a core crystal of a particular colour. Also included is a quick-fix exercise that will give you a general energy boost any time you are feeling physically drained or under par. And finally, we look at ways of tackling common types of "dis-ease" using the power of the crystals.

STRESS AND IMBALANCE
IN THE BODY

Why does our subtle energy system become imbalanced in the first place? One of the main contributors is stress, which can affect us energetically as well as emotionally and physically. Our stress response has evolved over thousands of years as a primitive physical reaction to a perceived threat. The body starts to pump out large amounts of adrenaline (epinephrine), which stimulates the heart to beat faster, sends more blood to the brain and prepares the muscles for "fight or flight".

Of course, in everyday life, it is unlikely that we will need to fight or flee from a predator, but the fast pace of modern life causes our bodies to react as if we do. And, as we are often unable to use up the extra adrenaline that we have produced, our body's natural balance is disturbed.

Practically everyone experiences stress at some time in their lives. Many aspects of modern Western life-styles are stressful. In the workplace meeting deadlines, negotiating deals and coping with difficult people can all cause stress. And our home environment can be a further source of worry, whether because of strained personal relationships, financial difficulties or the struggle to maintain a balance between our career and our family.

Stress can cause blockages in any or all of the chakras, depending on the type and its cause. For example, stress resulting from having your self-confidence undermined is likely to have a particularly negative effect on the solar plexus chakra.Working with crystals to unblock the chakras can help us to relax both physically and mentally, and release tension and anxiety.

Crystals with good stress-busting abilities include calming, soothing blue lace agate (see p.24); protective, restorative carnelian (see p.21); rose quartz (see p.23) for its gentle, comforting energy; amethyst (see p.26) for its all-round healing properties; and yellow jasper, which has a detoxifying effect, releases emotional blockages and helps to empower you. All you need to do is lie down and place your chosen anti-stress crystal on its associated chakra (see pp.44–5) for about 15 minutes or until you feel more calm and centred.

THE IMPORTANCE OF BEING GROUNDED

Most of us know what it's like to feel "ungrounded" — it is when we feel disorientated, or even disconnected from life. Crystal therapists believe that this is because our chakras are out of balance, disrupting the flow of our subtle energy. Conversely, when we feel grounded, we feel connected to everyone and everything, with a real sense of purpose and focus in life.

Working with crystals is a good way to regain ground-edness. For a quick fix, use stones linked with the base chakra, such as red jasper, which has intrinsic ground-ing qualities (see p.44). But, in the longer term, it's best to identify which chakra (or chakras) is out of balance and then choose appropriate crystals to work on it.

Each of the following visualizations rebalances a certain chakra using a certain crystal — use the headings to help you to select the best one for you. Or, look at the core crystal directory (pp.18–27), chakra summary (pp.44–5) or colour summary (pp.48–9) to assess which crystal, and therefore exercise, is most appropriate.

REALIZING YOUR GOALS
Base chakra: Red jasper

Sit somewhere comfortable and close your eyes. Take a minute to think about a goal, such as succeeding at a forthcoming job interview or finding a new home. Take three deep breaths, sighing out to release tension and to aid the grounding process. Open your eyes.

Take a piece of red jasper in your left (receiving) hand, and look closely at its colour, shape and texture. Close your eyes again and imagine that you can feel heat radiating from the crystal. Let the heat envelop you, and in your imagination, take yourself to a desert. Be aware of the heat and stillness all around you. As the sun sets, see the desert bathed in the red of your crystal. All is still and quiet. Let the colour gently surround your physical body. Connect with the primal energy of the desert and envisage your goal achieved and surrounded by it.

When you are ready, bring yourself back by focusing on the weight of your body as you sit, then become aware of your breathing and open your eyes.

FINDING CONTENTMENT
Sacral chakra: Carnelian

Sit somewhere comfortable, take a carnelian in your left (receiving) hand and look at it carefully. Close your eyes. Relax by breathing slowly and deeply.

Next, in your mind's eye, try to recall the colour and shape of the carnelian crystal. Then, envisage yourself standing in front of an orange door. Open the door and enter a room that is glowing with the flickering flames of a burning log fire. Go forward and sit in front of the fire. Watch the flames dancing contentedly and energetically around the pieces of wood in a range of orange hues.

Now feel the energy of the colours from the fire filling your aura. Experience the energy as heat, warming and energizing your sacral chakra, and intensifying the chakra's colour. Focus on happy times and give yourself permission to live vibrantly – like the flames.

In your own time, begin to focus again on your physical body and the noises in the room. Wriggle your fingers and toes and, when you are ready, open your eyes.

HARNESSING YOUR STRENGTH
Solar plexus chakra: Golden tiger's eye

Sit somewhere comfortable, close your eyes and hold a golden tiger's eye stone in your left (receiving) hand. Take three deep breaths and sigh to release tension.

Now imagine that you are standing in a white corridor outside a yellow door. Open the door and enter a room that is bright with sunlight. You are drawn to the window, and you sit nearby on a soft, yellow chair. Feel yourself sinking into the cushioned seat, which enfolds you in an empowering, invigorating yellow embrace.

You feel the sunlight warming your face as it streams in through the window. Looking outside, what do you see? Perhaps a field of golden wheat or yellow sunflowers? Or an orchard of lemon trees, heavy with brilliant yellow fruit? Draw the yellow energy in to your solar plexus chakra, just above the navel. Feel the warm glow there in your power centre become stronger and more vibrant.

When you are ready, focus on the weight of your body as you sit, breathe deeply, then open your eyes.

GIVING UNCONDITIONAL LOVE
Heart chakra: Rose quartz

Sit somewhere comfortable, close your eyes and relax. Take three deep breaths, exhaling any tension.

Place a rose quartz crystal on a table and gaze at it to explore its beauty. Try to connect with the rose quartz by visualizing energy flowing from your heart chakra to the crystal and back again in an energy circuit.

Imagine the pink energy from the rose quartz as a stream that cleanses your heart, soothing and uplifting your very being. You may see the rose quartz energy as a beautiful waterfall that washes away any stagnant energy held in the heart chakra. Feel yourself going into a deeper state of relaxation. Visualize the pink energy around your heart chakra expanding outward, and filling with thoughts and feelings of unconditional love for all your fellow human beings. Allow yourself to feel renewed, recharged and full of positive, loving thoughts.

Slowly bring your focus back to the room and, when you are ready, open your eyes.

FINDING YOUR OWN VOICE
Throat chakra: Blue lace agate

Sit somewhere comfortable, relax and close your eyes. Hold a blue lace agate stone in your left (receiving) hand. Take three deep breaths and sigh to release any tension.

Imagine yourself walking through a meadow of light blue flowers. It is a warm afternoon and the sky above you is a clear, piercing blue. You sit down among the flowers, sense their colour surrounding you and feel the softness of the petals enfolding you,

Breathe in deeply, allowing the light blue colour to pulsate in your throat chakra to boost your powers of self-expression. Breathe out as you imagine yourself releasing unspoken words and thoughts. As they float out, sense your subtle energy flowing more smoothly and trust that you will always find the words to express yourself clearly – at the right time and to the right person.

When you are ready, gently let the image fade and feel your awareness returning to the room. Focus on your breathing and, when you are ready, open your eyes.

GETTING IN TOUCH WITH YOUR INTUITION
Brow chakra: Sodalite

Sit comfortably with a sodalite crystal in your left (receiving) hand. Gaze into it and then close your eyes. Now, imagine yourself walking along a moonlit path under an indigo velvet sky. You come to the edge of a lake and see the shimmering reflection of the moon illuminating the stillness of the water.

You feel the cool night breeze and put on a rich indigo cloak that symbolizes intuitive wisdom, drawing it close to your body. Gaze awhile at the water and feel the spiritual energy envelop you. As you connect with the energy, focus on your brow chakra. Visualize an eye there and acknowledge the wise intuition within. (You may be aware of a physical tugging sensation, or see colours that move and change.) When you are ready, remove the cloak and retrace your steps to where you started.

Now gently let the scene fade and bring your attention back into the room. Become aware of your breathing and, when you are ready, open your eyes.

BECOMING SPIRITUALLY AWARE
Crown chakra: Amethyst

Sit comfortably, take an amethyst in your left (receiving) hand and relax. Breathe deeply and slowly. Feel the crystal becoming bigger and lighter, and imagine absorbing its purple energy into your aura.

Now, visualize your physical body becoming more ethereal. Draw the crystal's energy to the top of your head, to your crown chakra, and imagine a silver cord flowing out from your crown chakra into the universe. Feel yourself floating in space, surrounded by myriad twinkling, purple stars in an ocean of velvet blackness. Everything is connected and interrelated. You feel a wonderful sense of peace and oneness with the universe. Stay in that place as you experience a deep spiritual connection between your inner self and the universe.

Bring your focus gently back to your body and your breathing. Become aware of your feet touching the ground. Wiggle your fingers and toes and, when you are ready, open your eyes.

HARMONIZING YOUR CHAKRAS

If your energy reserves are low, or you feel that your body generally needs revitalizing, you can use the following crystal placement to rebalance all your chakras at the same time.

Lie down on the floor and ask a friend or family member to place the first seven core crystals on their corresponding chakra points (see pp.20–27), starting at the base chakra and finishing at the crown chakra. Once the crystals are in position, relax and close your eyes. Breathe deeply and slowly, then focus on each chakra in turn for at least a minute. Notice which chakras seem to draw more energy from their respective crystals. This will indicate which chakras are blocked or out of alignment, and are therefore most in need of work.

When you are ready, bring your focus back to your body and your breathing, then gently remove the crystals. You could give extra support to the chakras that need the most work by carrying their associated crystals around with you after the treatment.

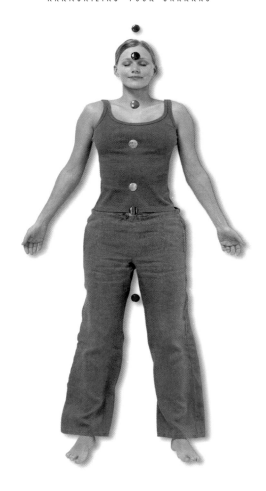

OVERCOMING "DIS-EASE"

Crystal therapists believe that many emotional or common physical problems and forms of "dis-ease" are simply a result of unaddressed energetic imbalances. Try using crystals to help you to overcome the following problems if they feature in your life.

A negative outlook Do you regard the "glass of life" as half empty or half full? People who maintain a positive attitude to life tend to achieve more, stay healthier and have more fun. If you find yourself feeling negative, citrine can help – carry a piece around, wear jewellery that contains it, or keep a large stone where you can see it to remind you to stay positive.

Long-term stress If we continually subject ourselves to anxiety and stress, it is likely that our physical health will eventually suffer. Some people develop digestive problems, some skin disorders, while others get depressed, suffer from headaches or cannot sleep. More seriously, the constant release of adrenaline and other stress-related chemicals can damage the heart.

To counteract stress, use crystals such as rose quartz, amethyst and blue lace agate. You can either keep them on your person or make a gem essence (see pp.56–7) to use when you feel particularly pressurized.

Weak immune system In today's hectic world, it can be difficult always to eat healthy food, relax and get enough sleep, and as a result we can weaken our immune system. Crystals that can boost this vital defence mechanism include green aventurine, blue lace agate and blood-stone. You can carry them around with you or wear jewellery that contains them.

Emotional shock and trauma It is essential for our well-being that we acknowledge and express shock or trauma. A good way to encourage this is to undergo a course of treatments with a crystal healer. You can also use a chakra layout (see pp.80–81) to support this process and to rebalance your subtle energy field.

Harmony is eating and resting,
sleeping and waking: balance in all you do.
This is the path to peace.

BHAGAVAD GITA

(1st or 2nd century)

With an eye made quiet by the power of
harmony, and the deep power of joy,
we see into the life of things.

WILLIAM WORDSWORTH

(1770–1850)

Chapter Four

directing
crystal energy

While we can use crystals to focus on individual chakras to empower us in myriad ways and to make our *chi* flow freely, we can also direct them to help us to overcome specific, negative emotional and mental states, and to set goals in our lives.

The body's subtle energy can be affected by all sorts of circumstances — from the everyday to the extraordinary — which can leave it drained and in need of replenishment. In this chapter, we start by exploring how crystals can protect our subtle energy from people or situations that sap it. We go on to present visualizations that will help to boost our physical energy – using amethyst and clear quartz, which are often used with the brow and crown chakras.

We then move on to use crystal placements, gem essences and further visualizations, as well as affirmations and meditations to aid us in improving particular aspects of our lives. Each exercise suggests specific crystals to work with, but you can select a different stone if you feel that it would work better for you. Choose from the range of exercises to help you to receive love and nurturing, set positive goals, boost your self-confidence, resolve problems, find clarity, tap in to calm and enhance your creativity.

PROTECTING YOUR ENERGY

Now that you have become more aware of your chakras and your subtle energy, you may feel increased sensitivity to people or situations that drain your energy.

Try to remember an occasion when you felt fine until you encountered a particular person and, despite having a normal conversation, you came away feeling drained and negative. This type of person can be called an "energy vampire", as they unwittingly draw on your *chi*.

It is possible to protect yourself against people draining your *chi* by carrying or wearing crystals with protective qualities. For example, carnelian provides a stronger boundary to the energy field of the person carrying it; both smoky quartz and clear quartz soak up negativity from others and transmute it into more positive feelings; and rose quartz counteracts negative energy by radiating compassion and love to bring peace. In circumstances when you have to deal with someone who is particularly hostile toward you, carry black tourmaline for strong protection against any ill wishes.

INCREASING YOUR ENERGY

This exercise will boost your physical energy levels as well as help your *chi* to flow more freely.

Sitting or lying down somewhere comfortable, hold a clear quartz crystal in your left (receiving) hand and an amethyst in your right (giving) hand. Visualize the clear quartz becoming softer and radiating white light. Next, imagine the white light traveling up your arm to your shoulder, where it flows to cleanse and harmonize every part of your physical and energetic body. Imagine the white light turning into pure energy everywhere it goes.

Then, activate the amethyst by imagining it pulsing in your right hand. Visualize it banishing all stagnant *chi*, then drawing the clear quartz energy toward it and radiating it outward to all areas of your physical and subtle body. In your mind's eye, see yourself totally immersed in the pure white energy.

When you feel physically recharged, take a few deep breaths and bring your focus gradually back to the room. Finally, cleanse both the crystals (see p.30).

RECEIVING LOVE AND NURTURING

This exercise utilizes the pink energy of rose quartz to support and nurture you. It provides a useful lift when you are feeling a little low, lonely or unloved.

Take six rose quartz crystals — small tumblestones are fine and inexpensive, although heart-shaped pieces make the exercise even more effective. Place the crystals in a large oval, with one above your head, one below your feet, and one each side of your shoulders and your calves. You can lay out the crystals before you lie down.

Then, lie inside the crystal layout and imagine each stone glowing with pink light. Envisage each crystal's energy slowly expanding until it all merges to form a pink cloud surrounding your body — a "bath" of pink energy radiating around you and through your aura. For as long as you wish, allow the pink energy to fill you with unconditional love and compassion.

When you are ready, take a few deep breaths and gradually bring your awareness back to the room. Remove the crystals and cleanse them (see p.30).

SETTING POSITIVE AIMS

One of the best ways to set yourself positive aims is to use affirmations. And holding or wearing crystals while you make statements of clear intent will give your affirmations extra power.

First, decide what you really want and which areas of your life you wish to work on. To clarify your desires, write them down and then incorporate them into affirmations. Place an appropriate crystal (see opposite) on the paper to further empower it.

Keep your affirmations simple, short and to the point. For example, if you'd like to restore your health, your affirmation could be: "I am healthy." Always use the present tense, because you want your wishes to manifest in the present. Use positive language – the whole point of using affirmations is to reprogramme your negative thought processes into positive ones. And believe that you can change yourself, or manifest what you ask for.

It's a good idea to set aside a time each day when you repeat your affirmation(s), with the appropriate crystal in place or in your hand. However, you can use affirmations whenever you find yourself thinking negatively.

To help you to improve specific areas of your life, try using the following affirmations and crystals.

Health I am healthy. I love and care for my body. I am always able to maintain my ideal weight. I am full of energy. *Suggested crystals*: blue lace agate, turquoise.

Self-esteem I deserve to be happy and successful. I can make my own choices. I deserve to be loved. I choose to be happy. I have the power to change myself. *Suggested crystals*: yellow jasper, golden tiger's eye.

Peace and harmony I am at peace. I forgive others. I am filled with the love of the universe. *Suggested crystals*: rose quartz, green aventurine.

Abundance I am successful in all that I do. Everything I do is rewarded. I always have sufficient money to meet my needs. *Suggested crystals*: red jasper, citrine.

BOOSTING SELF-CONFIDENCE

One of the best crystals to use for increasing self-confidence is golden tiger's eye. It is particularly effective when taken as a gem essence because, as with all crystals, its energy is enhanced during the essence's creation process. The sun imbues the crystal (and hence the essence) with assertive, masculine energy, which is excellent for supporting the solar plexus chakra when your self-confidence is low.

To make golden tiger's eye essence, simply leave the stone in a bowl of spring water – preferably in direct sunlight – for about six hours, and then remove it.

Take a couple of drops of gem essence two or three times a day under your tongue, or more often if required. Alternatively, keep the essence in a dropper bottle and simply add it to your bath water or a room spray when you need to boost your confidence. It is particularly helpful before and during stressful events, such as an important meeting or examination. At such times you can add a few drops to mineral water and sip it slowly.

RESOLVING PROBLEMS

When we are worried about a decision, or upset about a disagreement or simply in need of a fresh perspective on a matter, it can help if we "sleep on it". Often, the next day we can see a way forward that we hadn't thought of before. Sleeping with one or more crystals under your pillow can enhance this process.

Sodalite (see p.25) is a particularly good choice because it is a stone often linked with the brow chakra, which is the centre of intuition and creative thinking. It can support and encourage a clear mind on all levels, from the conscious to the subconscious.

Place your chosen crystal under your pillow before you go to sleep, lie back with your eyes closed and mentally ask the crystal to help you to resolve your problem or dilemma. Then, just go to sleep as usual.

Keep a pen and paper next to the bed, so that you can jot down in the morning any dreams or insights that you had during the night, before you forget them. Then analyze your notes. Does the answer lie within them?

FINDING CLARITY

Clear quartz has an energy that is good for bringing calm and clarity to situations. You can use this crystal whenever you are too agitated to think properly, or wish to release blocked energy that may be holding you back.

This visualization will restore harmony to each chakra in turn, giving you the ability to see any situation clearly. Sitting comfortably, hold a clear quartz in your left (receiving) hand. Close your eyes and visualize your breath drawing the energy from the quartz into your crown chakra. Imagine the clarifying energy swirling around and restoring your chakra to its perfect state. Repeat this process slowly, moving down through each chakra (see pp.42–3), finishing with the base chakra.

Once you have "cleared" all the chakras, visualize sending the quartz energy into your entire aura. See it whirling through the subtle bodies, refreshing and cleansing them. When you are ready, open your eyes and bring your focus back into the room. Watch your breathing for a minute or so to fully ground yourself.

TAPPING IN TO CALM

Relaxation and meditation techniques have many proven benefits. For example, they help to alleviate physical responses to stress by reducing high blood pressure; promote greater focus and concentration; encourage a positive state of mind; stimulate creativity; speed up the healing processes; and improve the functioning of the body. Interestingly, you can boost these benefits even further by using crystals when you practise relaxation and meditation techniques.

Crystals improve our ability to meditate and relax because they help to quieten the body, mind and emotions. Some of the best stones to use for this purpose are: blue lace agate, rose quartz and clear quartz. Amethyst is also excellent, as it works well with the crown chakra and has an overall calming and healing effect.

Try the following meditation. Sit somewhere comfortable where you will not be disturbed and hold your chosen crystal in your left (receiving) hand. Look closely at the stone, paying attention to its colour and texture.

Now close your eyes and feel the crystal merging into your hand and becoming part of you. If you feel a gentle pulsing from the stone, try to match your breathing to that frequency. If not, just breathe deeply and evenly.

Imagine the energy from the crystal expanding and, as you do so, feel your body becoming more and more relaxed. In your mind's eye see any physical tension or mental anxiety simply floating away, as you are supported in a cloud of energy the same colour as the crystal you are holding. Feel your body and mind releasing all your stresses.

When you are ready, visualize the crystal's energy simply draining away into the earth beneath your feet. Become aware of the stone taking form again in your hand. Slowly bring your mind back to reality and then ground yourself by focusing on your breathing for a few moments. When you are ready, open your eyes.

Practise this meditation for about 20 minutes if you are doing it at home. Or you can use it as a five-minute stress buster at your desk at work, or whenever you feel tension building.

AIDING EFFECTIVE COMMUNICATION

The throat chakra is associated with communication because it helps us to express our thoughts, feelings and opinions clearly and calmly.

One of the most effective stones for working with the throat chakra is blue lace agate. Native North Americans had a custom in which they used blue lace agate as a "talking stick" – during meetings, participants took turns to hold the stone when they had their say. Try using blue lace agate in this way during important discussions to help everyone to express their thoughts and opinions clearly, and to listen openly and attentively. Or, place a blue lace agate in a bowl of water in your living room or a meeting room at work to help discussions to proceed positively and productively.

Wearing a blue lace agate necklace can also help you to express your point of view plainly and persuasively, as well as to improve your self-expression through creativity. Try having one of these stones nearby when you are next writing, drawing or painting.

ENHANCING CREATIVITY

One of the best ways to use crystals to enhance creativity is to combine them in a pattern. You can do this intuitively by simply moving the stones around on a table until they form a pattern you like, or you can find a piece of patterned paper or fabric and place your crystals on it. Sit comfortably with your arrangement in front of you and gaze at the pattern. Look at the centre, then gradually allow your focus to drift outward. Allow the crystal pattern to fill your consciousness. When you are ready, slowly return your awareness to the room.

You can also try using your crystals with a mandala, which you can find in many meditation books. Mandalas are circular designs or patterns of images, which symbolize the universe and have been used by humankind since the earliest times as an aid to meditation. By placing crystals on mandalas for meditation, you stimulate the creative, right side of the brain. You can use any crystals, but aventurine, citrine, blue lace agate and clear quartz work particularly well.

Your treasure house is within:
it contains all that you'll ever need.

HUI-HAI

(720–814ce)

Look and you will find it —
what is unsought will go undetected.

SOPHOCLES

(c496–406bce)

expanding your work with crystals

So far in this book we have looked at ways of using crystal therapy to treat and balance our own physical and subtle bodies. However, crystals are also the perfect choice for optimizing our environment, as their mere presence in a room can help to enhance the energetic state of anyone (and anything) present, thus boosting the well-being of not only ourselves, but also of family, friends and colleagues.

In this chapter, we look beyond the self. We start by focusing on how we can harness the power of crystals in the home, whether to use them to change the atmosphere in a particular room or to nurture and heal those close to us – for example, our children and pets. We then move on to learn how to use crystals to improve the atmosphere in our workplace and our efficiency in the work we do.

For centuries crystals have been immensely popular as gifts, so we also include a list of birthstones, the gems linked to each month of the year, and a list of stones associated with the signs of the Zodiac to help you to choose appropriate gifts.

And finally, we discuss how crystals can be used with many other complementary therapies to enhance and amplify their effect.

CRYSTALS IN THE HOME

Just as crystals can send out specific healing energies to the body, so, too, can they radiate healing energies into their immediate environment. Try focusing your crystals' energy in your home by putting them in specific rooms for specific purposes (see pp.52–3). For example, to generate unconditional love in the bedroom, place a large chunk of rose quartz on the bedside table; to promote an atmosphere of lively optimism in the dining room, place a bowl of yellow jasper there; and to improve your telephone communication skills, put some blue lace agate stones by the phone. However, do remember to cleanse your crystals regularly (see pp.30–31) when you use them in this way, because they will absorb energy from all the people who use the room.

You can also change the atmosphere in a room by spraying it with a gem essence (see pp.56–7) further diluted with spring water. For example, to cleanse the room of a negative atmosphere, use the essences of crystals such as clear quartz or black tourmaline. You can amplify the effect by mixing the gem essence with a few drops of cleansing essential oil, such as juniper, sage or frankincense. As you spray, concentrate on the corners, windows and doors of the room. If you don't have a spray bottle, try placing a few drops of a gem essence in the palm of one hand and clapping your hands around the room. This is a really powerful way to clear stagnant energy and lift the energetic vibration in the room.

Another option is to create your own sacred space where you can sit quietly and say your affirmations or work with your crystals. Some people set up an altar — not necessarily using religious artifacts, but rather items that generate energies appropriate for them, such as putting a crystal on top of the picture of a loved one who currently needs extra support. This can act as a focal point for you to use when you wish to send loving, positive thoughts either to yourself, friends or family, or even the world. You could also use a bowl of spring water, perhaps with a beautiful flower and some gem essences placed in it, to support the intent that you are working with at that time.

CHILDREN AND CRYSTALS

Children respond especially well to crystals, because they have a more vibrant subtle energy system than adults and have had less time to be affected by life's challenging experiences. This means that they are highly sensitive to crystal energies. Allow your child to select his or her own crystal, as children are extremely intuitive, so they are usually drawn to the stone that is right for them.

For children under five, use a gem essence (see pp.56–7), as there is no danger of them swallowing the stone. You can rub the essence into your child's skin, put a few drops in their bath water or in their drink, or add the essence to the water when you wash your child's clothes. Alternatively, put the crystal in a bowl of water and leave it in your child's room, out of his or her reach.

Crystals can offer support to older children on issues, such as bullying, lack of confidence, hyperactivity, difficulty sleeping, exam worries, and so on. However, never use crystals as a substitute for medical treatment – always consult your doctor if your child is ill.

PETS AND CRYSTALS

Animals, like humans, have a subtle energy field that includes chakras, an aura and meridians. They are also sensitive to crystal energies. Try an experiment with your pet. Lay out some crystals on the floor and see which stones it goes to and which it avoids. You can also place bowls of water energized with different crystals for your pet to drink from, and see if it has a preference. As with humans, it will be drawn instinctively to stones that can give it healing.

Place a stone that your pet seems to like in its usual sleeping place, such as its basket, or attach a small crystal to its collar. However, do ensure that the animal won't be able to swallow the crystal or hurt itself on it. Alternatively, if you have a tumblestone, you can always gently rub the stone on its fur or coat. When the healing is working well, your pet will relax and respond positively, but if it seems uncomfortable or stressed in any way, remove the crystal at once. Always take your pet to a vet if you have any concerns about its health.

CRYSTALS IN THE WORKPLACE

Crystals can increase your effectiveness at work and harmonize negative office energies. Place a citrine on your desk to enliven you and to help create abundance, or keep a bowl of mixed tumblestones and select the appropriate crystal when you need support.

To Counteract Workplace Radiation

All sorts of office equipment, such as computers, photo-copiers, printers, and even lighting, give off low levels of radiation. As we add more equipment to our work space, the radiation levels can become detrimental to us. Many crystal healers recommend putting rose quartz, amethyst or black tourmaline on or around your desk or seating area to absorb and counteract electromagnetic energy.

To Help with Presentations and Interviews

If your work involves giving presentations or meeting new people, wear or carry a crystal such as blue lace agate or turquoise to improve effective communication.

To Relieve Stress

If you have tight deadlines or find that you are becoming increasingly stressed at work, tap into the energies of amethyst to calm you, or use clear quartz to provide clear sightedness. Simply hold the crystal and close your eyes. Breathe in deeply through your nose and out through your mouth as you draw upon the crystal's energy.

To Encourage Assertiveness

In situations where you need to be assertive – for example when asking for a pay rise, or giving or receiving an appraisal – use yellow jasper to help to support personal power. Visualize breathing its energy deeply into your solar plexus area. Alternatively, use red jasper to keep you grounded and focused.

To Protect Yourself from Others' Negativity

A clash of personalities in the workplace can create negative energy. Use carnelian to protect against people who "drain" you. Or if someone acts as if they dislike you, use black tourmaline to dispel their ill-wishes.

CRYSTALS AS GIFTS: BIRTHSTONES

Traditionally, certain crystals have been associated with particular months of the year. Known as birthstones, these crystals can make beautiful, useful gifts, whether as tumblestones, ornaments or set in jewellery.

The months and their associated birthstones are:

January – Garnet
February – Amethyst
March – Aquamarine
April – Diamond
May – Emerald
June – Pearl
July – Ruby
August – Peridot
September – Sapphire
October – Opal
November – Topaz
December – Turquoise

As well as the birthstones listed opposite, there are crystals associated with the astrological signs. These are known as Zodiac birthstones, and you can use them for support in difficult circumstances, or to help you to develop the natural gifts that are particularly associated with your star sign.

The Zodiac birthstones are:

Aquarius (21 January–18 February): Garnet, amethyst

Pisces (19 February–20 March): Amethyst, aquamarine

Aries (21 March–20 April): Bloodstone, diamond

Taurus (21 April–21 May): Sapphire, amber

Gemini (22 May–22 June): Agate, chrysoprase

Cancer (23 June–22 July): Emerald, moonstone

Leo (23 July–23 August): Onyx, carnelian

Virgo (24 August–22 September): Carnelian, jade

Libra (23 September–23 October): Peridot, lapis lazuli

Scorpio (24 October–22 November): Beryl, apache tear

Sagittarius (23 November–21 December): Topaz, amethyst

Capricorn (22 December–20 January): Ruby, agate

CRYSTALS AND OTHER THERAPIES

Crystals lend themselves perfectly to enhancing almost any complementary therapy. Many practitioners who work with the subtle energy system, such as acupuncturists, reflexologists, massage therapists and reiki healers, use crystals in their treatments. For example, some acupuncturists employ crystal points, rather than needles, to stimulate the flow of subtle energy, particularly in children. Reflexologists and massage therapists use crystals and massage stones respectively to amplify the effect of their treatment, while reiki healers utilize crystals both to make their treatments more powerful and to give to clients for self-healing at home.

Even beauty spas and salons now incorporate crystals into a range of treatments. For example, in hot stone therapy, basalt – a form of crystalline volcanic rock – is placed on the client's chakra points to clear energy blockages before massage commences.

Many different kinds of therapists also use crystals in the therapy room to create the right atmosphere, without incorporating them into the treatment itself. For example, placing rose quartz under a therapist's couch or in another appropriate area, will generate a loving, nurturing feel in the treatment room; or placing carnelian in the room protects the therapist so that they do not become drained during the treatment.

Anyone wishing to incorporate crystals into their treatments should ensure that they get adequate training in the practice, because the strong spiritual connection and potent effect that crystals sometimes have, can cause surprisingly powerful responses. It is therefore imperative that practitioners of other therapies are able to explain to the client what is happening to them, and to offer them adequate support and advice.

Although crystals are excellent energy-balancers and -enhancers, their incorporation into other treatments tends to boost the power of the treatment and thus increase the possibility of a client experiencing a "healing reaction". During this time, a client's symptoms may temporarily worsen (though usually only for a couple of days), before improving.

His high endeavours are an inward light
That makes the path before him always bright.

WILLIAM WORDSWORTH

(1770–1850)

By meditation upon light and upon radiance,
knowledge of the spirit can be reached
and peace can be achieved.

PATANJALI

(2ND CENTURY BCE)

INDEX

affirmations, 50, 94–5
agate, blue lace, 24
  aiding communication,
    105
  rebalancing chakras, 63,
    74
amethyst, 26, 31
  increasing energy, 91
  rebalancing chakras, 63,
    78
apophyllite, 25
aquamarine, 24
aura, 11, 36, 39, 43
aventurine, green, 23
  rebalancing chakras, 63

base chakra, 44
  rebalancing, 66
Benveniste, Jacques, 56
Bible, 14
birthstones, 120–1
breathing, 51, 53
brow chakra, 45
  rebalancing, 77

calcite
  blue, 24
  green, 23
  orange, 21
calming meditation, 102–3
carnelian, 21

grounding quality, 65
  rebalancing chakras, 63,
    69
celestite, 26
chakras, 11, 36, 43–5
  balancing, 46, 60–83
chi, 11
  chakras, 43
  discovering, 40
  protecting, 88
  rebalancing, 36, 39
  see also energy
children, 115
chunks, crystal, 16
citrine, 22, 54
clarity, finding, 100
clusters, crystal, 16–17
colour
  associations, 48–9
  choosing crystals, 28–9
communication, aiding, 105
complementary therapies,
  122–3
contentment, reaching, 69
creativity, enhancing, 106
crown chakra, 45
  rebalancing, 78
crystal therapists, 10–11,
  32–3
crystals
  care of, 30–1

children and, 115
choosing, 28–9
cleansing, 30
colours, 46–9
and complementary
  therapies, 122–3
core crystal directory,
  18–27
energy, 10, 36
formation of, 12
forms, 16–17
gem essences, 56–7,
  112–13, 115
hardness ratings, 18, 31
history of, 14–15
in the home, 112–13
pets and, 116
placements, 54
in the workplace,
  118–19

diamond, Herkimer, 27

Egypt, ancient, 14–15
Emoto, Dr Masaru, 56
energy
  chakras, 43
  directing crystal energy,
    86–107
  enhancing crystal energy,
    50–51

experiencing crystal
energy, 52–3
increasing your own, 91
protecting, 88
see also chi; subtle energy
system

gem essences, 56–7, 112–13,
115
goals, realizing, 66
Greece, ancient, 15
groundedness, 65

hardness ratings, 18, 31
heart chakra, 45
rebalancing, 73
hematite, 20
Hill, Sir John, 15
history of crystals, 14–15
home, crystals in, 112–13

incense, smudging, 30
intent, 50
intuition, getting in touch
with, 77
Islam, 14

jasper, red, 20
grounding quality, 65
rebalancing chakras, 66
jasper, yellow, 22
rebalancing chakras, 63

lapis lazuli, 25

love
receiving, 92
unconditional, 73, 112

meditation, calming, 102–3
meridians, 11, 36, 39
Mohs Scale, 18, 31
moonstone, 21

pendulums, crystal, 11
pets, 116
placements, 54

quartz, cleansing, 30
quartz, clear, 27
finding clarity, 100
increasing energy, 91
quartz, rose, 23, 31
"bath" grid, 54
rebalancing chakras,
63, 73
receiving love, 92
quartz, smoky, 20

radiation, office equipment,
118
relaxation, 102–3

sacral chakra, 44
rebalancing, 69
selenite, 26
self-confidence,
boosting, 96
self-treatment, 32–3

sodalite, 25
rebalancing chakras, 77
resolving problems, 99
solar plexus chakra, 44
rebalancing, 70
storing crystals, 31
strength, harnessing, 70
stress
calming meditation, 102–3
effects of, 60–63, 82–3
relieving, 119
subtle energy system, 11
in animals, 116
crystal placements, 54
rebalancing, 36, 62
see also chi

throat chakra, 45
aiding communication,
105
rebalancing, 74
tiger's eye, golden, 22
boosting self-confidence,
96
rebalancing chakras, 70
tumblestones, 17

visualization, 51, 53
directing crystal energy,
86–107
Vogel, Marcel, 15
voice, finding your own, 74

workplace crystals, 118–19

Picture Credits

The publisher would like to thank the following organizations and photographic libraries for permission to reproduce their material. Every care has been taken to trace copyright holders. However, if we have omitted anyone we apologize and will, if informed, make corrections to any future edition.

Page 13 Kevin Lang/Alamy, **34** Laurance B Aiuppy/Taxi/Getty Images, **38** Rob Howard/Corbis, **47** Photos.com, **58** Ken Graham/Stone/Getty Images, **64** JTB Photo/Photolibrary.com, **67** Alan Kearney/Taxi/Getty Images, **68** Mark Lewis/Stone/Getty Images, **71** Holger Leue/Look/Getty Images, **72** Stuart Westmorland/Stone/Getty Images, **75** Charles Krebs/Corbis, **76** Joseph Squillante/Photonica/Getty Images, **79** Image Pro 34/Dance and Jump Software, **84** Patricia de la Rosa/Stone/Getty Images, **98** Jerome Tisne/Iconica/Getty Images, **104** Studio MPM/Iconica/Getty Images, **108** Photos.com, **114** Michael Melford/National Geographic/Getty Images, **117** Tony Latham/Photolibrary.com, **124** Photos.com.

Author's Acknowledgments

My thanks to Sally for her steadfast support
and to Phil who inspires me more than
he realizes.

Thank you to Crystal Creations, who
supplied the crystal bracelets that were
photographed.

Publisher's Acknowledgments

The publishers would like to thank:
Model: Kate Mahoney
Make-up artist: Gilly Popham

Contact the author at:

www.lucisgroup.com